The Healing Hands of Jesus
"At sunset all those who had
friends suffering from diseases of
one kind or another brought
them to Him, and laying
His hands on each He cured them:
Luke 4, 40-11

"My dear child
I was condemned,
You are condemned.
We walk the way of the cross together."
(pause)

First Station

Jesus is Condemned
To Death

"*Lord Jesus, open my hands and
my heart to receive the
cross that is given to me.*"
(pause)

Second Station

Jesus receives
His Cross

"When I fall, Lord
Help me up again
Painful though it be,
To walk with you"
(pause)

Third Station

Jesus Falls
the First Time

*"Jesus reach out healing hands
to me as you did to your Mother.
Help me to reach out healing
hands to those around me."*

(pause)

Fourth Station

Jesus Meets
His Mother

"Thank you, Lord
For all those like Simon
Who help me to carry
My cross daily."
(pause)

Fifth Station

Simon Helps Jesus
To Carry the Cross

*"Thank you, Lord for family
and friends, doctors and nurses
and all who are kind to me
as Veronica was to you."*
(pause)

Sixth Station

*Veronica wipes the
Face of Jesus*

"Lord Jesus
Never let me give way
to depression or discouragement.
Lift me up again."
(pause)

Seventh Station

Jesus falls the
Second Time

*"Don't allow self pity
to turn me in on myself.
But make me conscious
of those who are worse off
than I am."*
(pause)

Eight Station

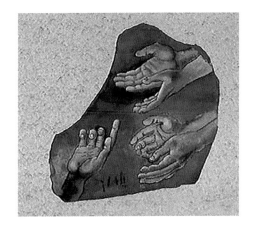

Jesus Consoles the
Women of Jerusalem

"Here I am again Lord
At a low ebb in my life
Your strength and courage
To go on, gives me
Strength and courage."
(pause)

Ninth Station

Jesus Falls the
Third Time

"Jesus help me to bear shame
and humiliation with the
dignity and self composure that
I see in you when they tore
your clothes from your body."
(pause)

Tenth Station

Jesus is stripped of
His Garments

"When I feel like running away
Help me to remember that you
Freely chose never to be
Separated from the cross."
(pause)

Eleventh Station

*Jesus is Nailed
to the Cross*

"Dear Jesus, one day I too will die like you. Don't allow me to fear death, but help me to know that on that day I will meet you face to face."

(pause)

Twelfth Station

*Jesus Dies
on the Cross*

"My sufferings too will end.
On that day I will be
separated from my cross
and I will rest with
you in Mary's arms."
(pause)

Thirteenth Station

Jesus is Taken Down
From the Cross

"And now I am content
to rest in the darkness,
because I know that you,
dear Jesus, are there with me."
(pause)

Fourteeth Station

Jesus is laid
in the Tomb

"Glory be to the Father
and to the Son,
and to the Holy Spirit
for all eternity.
Amen."

Fifteenth Station

Jesus is Risen

Artist,; Riccardo Caffi,
Original: Way of the Cross
Passionist Church,
Forest Hill,
Gaborone Botswana.